A Basic Guide To
CYCLING

An Official U.S. Olympic Committee
Sports Series

The U.S. Olympic Committee

Publishing
le, California

Editorial Statement

In the interest of brevity, the Editors have chosen to use the standard
English form of address. Please be advised that this usage is not meant
to suggest a restriction to, nor an endorsement of, any individual or
group of individuals, either by age, gender, or athletic ability. The
Editors certainly acknowledge that boys and girls, men and women, of
every age and physical condition are actively involved in sports and
we encourage everyone to enjoy the sports of his or her choice.

10 9 8 7 6 5 4 3 2 1

ISBN 1-882180-51-8

Additional Olympic-related materials are available from Griffin Publishing.

Griffin Publishing

544 W. Colorado Street
Glendale, California 91204

Telephone: 1-818-244-1470

Manufactured in the United States of America

Acknowledgments

PUBLISHER

Robert M. Howland
President, Griffin Publishing Group

USOC

United States Olympic Committee

John Krimsky, Jr
Deputy Secretary General

Barry King
Mike Moran
Bob Paul

SERIES EDITOR

Richard D. Burns, Ph.D.

WRITER

Joey Lorraine Parker

PRODUCTION EDITOR

Marjorie L. Marks

BOOK DESIGN

Mark M. Dodge

COORDINATOR

Robin L. Howland

CONSULTING EDITOR

Bob Mathias

CONTRIBUTING EDITORS

USA Cycling
United States Cycling Federation (USCF)
U.S. Pro (U.S. Professional Racing Association)
National Off-Road Bicycle Association (NORBA)

PHOTOS

USOC
USA Cycling, Inc.
Tandem Club of America
New England Cycling Support Association
Sandra Applegate

COVER PHOTO

USOC

The United States Olympic Committee

The U.S. Olympic Committee (USOC) is the custodian of the U.S. Olympic Movement and is dedicated to providing opportunities for American athletes of all ages.

The USOC, a streamlined organization of member organizations, is the moving force for support of sports in the United States that are on the program of the Olympic and/or Pan American Games, or those wishing to be included.

The USOC has been recognized by the International Olympic Committee since 1894 as the sole agency in the United States whose mission involves training, entering and underwriting the full expenses for the United States teams in the Olympic and Pan American Games. The USOC also supports the bid of U.S. cities to host the winter and summer Olympic Games, or the winter and summer Pan American Games and, after reviewing all the candidates, votes on and may endorse one city per event as the U.S. bid city. The USOC also approves the U.S. trial sites for the Olympic and Pan American Games team selections.

On behalf of the United States Olympic Committee,

Welcome to the
Olympic Sports Series

We are extremely pleased to inaugurate the Olympic Sports Series. I feel this unique series will encourage parents, athletes of all ages, and novices who are thinking about a sport for the first time, to get involved with the challenging and rewarding world of Olympic sports.

This series of paperback books covers both summer and winter sports, features Olympic history and basic sports fundamentals, and encourages family involvement. Each book includes information on how to get started in a particular sport, including appropriate equipment and clothing; rules of the game; health and fitness; basic first aid; and guidelines for spectators. Of special interest is the information on opportunities for senior citizens, volunteers and physically challenged athletes. In addition, each book is enhanced by photographs and illustrations and a complete, easy-to-understand glossary.

Because this family-oriented series neither assumes nor requires prior knowledge of a particular sport, it can be enjoyed by all age groups. Regardless of one's level of sports knowledge, playing experience or athletic ability, this official U.S. Olympic Committee Sports Series will encourage understanding and participation in sports and fitness.

The purchase of these books assists the U.S. Olympic Team. This series supports the Olympic mission and serves importantly to enhance participation in the Olympic and Pan American Games.

John Krimsky, Jr.
Deputy Secretary General

Contents

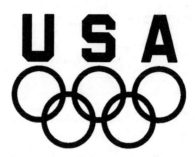

An Athlete's Creed

The most important thing in the Olympic Games is not to win but to take part, just as the most important thing in life is not the triumph but the struggle. The essential thing is not to have conquered but to have fought well.

These famous words, commonly referred to as the Olympic Creed, were once spoken by Baron Pierre de Coubertin, founder of the modern Olympic Games. Whatever their origin, they aptly describe the theme behind each and every Olympic competition.

CYCLING IN
THE OLYMPIC GAMES

Today, cycling is one of the most technically advanced sports in Olympic competition. Bicycle design and construction are constantly subjected to technological improvements, which are apparent with each passing year. No modern cyclist, nor cycling fan for that matter, would consider the lumbering machines of the 1900 Paris Games as adequate for competitive cycling. Yet cycling owes a great deal to those brave pioneers of the sport who started cycling on its way to becoming an international sport of champions.

Cycling struggled through a difficult growth period before reaching the Olympic superstar status it enjoys today. At the Paris Olympic Games in 1900, there was only one cycling event. Little was recorded about that event, suggesting—perhaps surprisingly in view of its popularity at the turn of the century—that cycling was not considered a primary Olympic sport.

The situation looked a little brighter for the St. Louis Games in 1904 when seven track races were included in the program as exhibition events; but no nations other than the United States participated in the cycling events. If that weren't bad enough, fewer than a handful of spectators showed up to watch them.

It appeared that the London Games in 1908 would be a step forward in terms of organization and participation. Track events were scheduled to be held on a banked 500-meter oval inside the main Olympic stadium, thereby allowing an increased number of spectators to attend the cycling competition. Moreover, organizers thought that holding cycling inside the main stadium, where newspapermen could be seated comfortably, would practically guarantee expanded, more favorable press coverage. Unfortunately, by the time of the competition, the weather had turned very bad, and spectators stayed away in droves. The competition was held on schedule, but the track surface was wet and slippery, causing many cyclists to slip, slide and crash. This did not improve the already skeptical media impression of cycling as an Olympic sport, and there was even talk of dropping cycling from future Olympic programs. Fortunately, cooler heads prevailed and cycling has seen steady growth and support in every Olympics since the wet and slippery Games of 1908.

At present, Olympic cycling consists of two separate categories of racing: track and road. Track races are held on steeply banked tracks called *velodromes*. Road racing is exactly what the name implies—racing on paved roadways. Mountain bike racing made its debut at the 1996 Olympic Games in Atlanta, Georgia, bringing a third dimension to cycling: off-road racing.

Photo courtesy of USOC

Olympic track racing is held on steeply-banked velodromes

Track bikes have no brakes and only one gear, which is adjusted according to the riding style of the cyclist and the size of the track. Road bikes are built with sophisticated aerodynamic shifting and braking qualities, and some have as many as 16 gears.

Spectator's Guide

The following spectator guidelines certainly apply to Olympic racing strategies and techniques, but also may be relevant for other top caliber events, such as the Tour de France, Pan American Games, and world cycling championships.

At the world championships, professionals and amateurs compete separately for the road race title, while at the national championships professionals and amateurs compete against one another for one title. In 1996, professionals were allowed to compete in cycling in the Olympic Games. If you are fortunate enough to attend a cycling competition, remember to stay well off the path and allow all riders plenty of room. This is especially important in off-road (or mountain bike) racing where path boundaries may be harder to define. Cyclists love to have spectators cheer them on, but not if they get in their way.

Road Races

Road races are mass start events that take place on paved roads. They can be point-to-point races over several days or long loops of five to twenty-five miles in length. Endurance is the main factor in road racing; distances of 100 miles and more for men, and 50 miles for women are not uncommon. Moreover, the topography (geographic features of an area or district) may vary from hilly to flat, then hilly again. Each of these features appeals to a particular type of cyclist. For example, usually lean, lightweight climbers prefer racing over the hilly portions of a course, but heavier, more powerful cyclists usually excel on the flat portions of a course. Endurance specialists often force the pace at the front of the pack, while the cyclists deliberately trail, waiting and watching for the opportune moment to burst forward and place themselves in the most advantageous position.

Watch for strong, aggressive riders to *attack* the group in an attempt to *break away* and head out on their own. Because a group can ride faster and with less effort than a soloist can, savvy riders know when—and when not—to employ the individual breakaway technique. If a lone rider runs into strong headwinds or crosswinds, or encounters a difficult hill, the "advantage" of being out front all alone will quickly become a major liability.

Photo courtesy of USOC

Road races are mass events that take place on paved roads.

Another type of breakaway you may see is the *cluster* break in which a number of riders surge forward, forming their own *paceline*. A cluster of riders has a better chance of success, particularly if the cluster contains several riders from a single team. The tip-off is to watch for riders wearing the same jersey. These riders will take turns setting the pace and resting in the draft. Riders from other teams may try to "sit in," refusing to take a turn at the front, or take a shorter turn than the others. The strategy is to try and slow the break, hoping one's own teammates can catch up, or a "maverick" rider may employ this technique to move close to the front while conserving energy for a final burst of speed to the finish line.

Watch the front of the main pack. If its leaders wear the same jersey as the breakaway riders, they are *blocking*, trying to keep the pack from chasing the breakaway group. If the leaders of the main pack are wearing jerseys different from those in the group break, a full-scale chase may be developing. Under these conditions, you may well see many lead changes before anyone crosses the finish line. Keep an eye out for the *sprinters*—this is when they make their move to the front.

Track Races

Racing in the velodromes requires a special bike and some equally special skills. Velodromes are not all the same. Some have very gentle banking, some are very steep. Some are elongated with sharp turns, while others are almost round with short straightaways.

All have lines painted on the track's surface. The blue line on the inside of the track marks the track's inner boundary. The sprinter's lane lies between this blue line and a thin red line, higher up on the track. A rider within this area is said to "own the lane," and may only be passed by a competitor who goes up and over. The uppermost thin blue line, called the stayer's line, marks the boundary between faster and slower traffic, with the faster riders below and slower riders above.

Photo courtesy of USOC

Track racing bikes, such as the one ridden here by U.S. Olympian Rebecca Twigg, have no brakes!

Olympic Track Events
Match Sprints
The match sprint event covers a distance of 1,000 meters, although timing does not begin until one or more of the riders crosses the 200 meter mark before the finish line. Typically,

two riders compete against each other at a time. Usually, riders perform "flying 200s" individually at the beginning of competition to determine who will sprint against whom. Match sprint events typically are games of "cat and mouse," where riders attempt to outwit each other for the best position during the first two laps. In addition to outstanding speed and power, the element of surprise and excellent bike handling skills are characteristics of match sprinters.

Points Race

The points race is the longest of all the Olympic track events, usually exceeding 40 kilometers (25 miles). Riders "sprint" for points every five laps, and usually the top four riders who cross the start/finish line first receive points. Point sprints in the middle of the race and on the last lap are worth double points. One way to win the points race, obviously, is to accumulate the most points, but another way is to "lap" the field. Riders who lap the field are scored ahead of riders with points. Characteristics of successful points racers include good sprinting ability, outstanding endurance, and excellent tactical skills.

Time Trials

Time trials are races against the clock. The rider with the fastest time is the winner. The Kilometer time trial and the Individual Pursuit are individual events, whereas the Team Pursuit is a team event.

Kilometer

The Kilometer time trial is 1,000 meters long, and riders start from a standstill. Because riders are forced to perform at a maximum effort for more than one minute, many people believe this event is one of the most challenging and stressful in track racing. Characteristics of successful kilometer riders include strength, power, and the ability to withstand high levels of stress.

Individual Pursuit

The Individual Pursuit is a longer time-trial type event, with men covering distances of 4,000 meters and women covering distances of 3,000 meters. Riders start Pursuit from a standstill, and two riders usually compete at the same time, starting on opposite sides of the track. Some events are structured so that riders qualify on time, even if they do not "catch" the opposing rider. At other events, a rider wins by "catching" the opposing rider.

Characteristics of successful pursuit riders include outstanding endurance and excellent pacing ability.

Team Pursuit
In the Team Pursuit, teams of four riders compete as units against other teams for the best time. In addition, the clock does not stop until the third rider crosses the start/finish line. Teams must work together so that weaker riders are not dropped. In addition to the endurance and pacing ability, team pursuit riders must have the ability to work together as a unit. In all other respects, the Team Pursuit is identical to the Individual Pursuit.

Off-Road Races
In the United States, the National Off-Road Bicycle Association (NORBA), a division of the U.S. Cycling Federation, is the governing body for the sport of mountain bike racing. NORBA sanctions racing and touring events throughout the 50 states, and promotes the sport internationally. Cycling made its Olympic debut at the Atlanta Games in 1996. Mountain biking is one of the fastest-growing cycling disciplines. NORBA now has more than 30,000 active members.

At the international level, mountain bike racing was first accepted by the *Federal International Amateur de Cyclisme* (FIAC)—the world governing body of cycling—in 1990. Its popularity has grown so large that mountain biking now has two World Championship events: downhill and cross-country. The downhill is a time-trial event designed to reward the fastest downhill bike racer—on a rather steep hill. A downhill specialist has to be daring and a superb bike handler. For spectators, this is an exciting event, since the action is fast and the rules are straightforward. The scoring is direct and uncomplicated, and the entire event takes place within viewing range.

The basic form of mountain bike racing is the cross-country event, held on an off-road course ranging from four to 20 miles in length. Riders face a variety of natural hazards such as sandy slopes, grassy knolls, steep mountains, streams and rivers, bogs and marshes. Mountain bikers tackle whatever crosses their path. It's hard to see the entire course, but spectators usually like to stand near a stream or hill where different riders make different decisions about how to traverse that hazard. As a result, spectators get to see a greater variety of off-road techniques.

Race times vary according to ability. Beginners usually can finish their course in one hour or less, while the longer pro races may take up to three hours or more.

There are two fundamental rules for mountain bike racing. First, bikes must have wheels no larger than 26 inches, with tires no thinner than 1.5 inches; plugged handlebars; and two independent brakes. Second, each rider must be self-sufficient—no outside assistance or technical support is allowed. (Contrast this with road racers who usually have elaborate support staffs accompanying them.) The idea behind off-road racing is that every competitor should (and does) have the same chance. The rider who can afford to buy umpteen bikes has no advantage over the rider who has only one bike. In off-road racing, participants finish the race on the bike they began with; substitutions are not allowed. If your bike becomes damaged beyond your ability to make immediate repairs, better luck next weekend. All competitors carry spare inner tubes and tire patches and change all flats themselves, but the winner ultimately is the one who is best able to keep his or her bike out of serious trouble.

Recent American Cycling Results

1995 World Championships

Individual Pursuit
Rebecca Twigg   First

Olympic Sprint
Bill Clay, Marty Nothstein,
Erin Hartwell   Third

Team Pursuit
Zach Conrad, Kirk Copeland,
Mariano Friedick, Matt Hamon,
Adam Laurent, Mike McCarthy   Third

Kilometer Time Trial
Erin Hartwell   Third

Junior Cross-Country
Cecilia Potts   Third

Veteran Cross-Country
Carol Waters   First

Veteran Cross-Country
Lisa Lamoreaux   Second

Senior Downhill
Leigh Donovan   First

Senior Downhill
Mike King   Third

Veteran Downhill
Bernard Unhassobiscay   Second

1995 World Cup

Mountain Bike Cross-Country
Juliana Furtado   First

U.S Olympic Cycling Medal Highlights

Event/Athlete	*Medal*
1912 Stockholm, Sweden	
Individual Road Race (Men)	
Carl Schutte	Bronze
1984 Los Angeles, USA	
Individual Pursuit (Men)	
Steve Hegg	Gold
Leonard Nitz	Bronze
Individual Road Race (Men)	
Alexi Grewal	Gold
Individual Road Race (Women)	
Connie Carpenter-Phinney	Gold
Rebecca Twigg	Silver
Team Pursuit (Men)	
Dave Grylls, Steve Hegg, Pat McDonough, L. Nitz	Silver
Match Sprint (Men)	
Mark Gorski	Gold
Nelson Vails	Silver
Team Time Trail (Men)	
Ron Kiefel, Roy Knickmann, Davis Phinney, Andy Weaver	Bronze
1988 Seoul, Korea	
Match Sprint (Women)	
Connie Paraskevin Young	Bronze

1992 Barcelona, Spain

Individual Pursuit (Women)
Rebecca Twigg   Bronze
1,000-Meter Time Trial (Men)
Erin Hartwell   Bronze

1996 Atlanta, Georgia

Cross Country Mountain Bike (Women)
Susan De Matti   Bronze
Kilometer Time Trial (Men)
Erin Hartwell   Silver
Match Sprint (Men)
Marty Northstein   Silver

A BRIEF HISTORY OF CYCLING

History indicates that the first functioning bicycle was designed in the 15th century by master craftsman and artisan Leonardo da Vinci. It was an odd-looking contraption, driven by cranks and pedals and held together with connecting rods. The first machine to resemble the contemporary bicycle was designed in France in the late 18th century. Known as the *celerifere*, this vehicle consisted of a wooden horse-shaped frame mounted on two wheels, propelled by the rider's feet. It was a cumbersome thing and difficult to mobilize, but it marked the beginning of modern bicycle construction.

Nearly 20 years later, Baron Karl von Mannheim designed a "bicycle" with steering, which quickly became nicknamed the "dandy-horse." It wasn't too dandy for the French postal service, however, which used it to deliver mail in the countryside. Kirkpatrick McMillan, a Scot, put pedals and connecting rods together, and the result was an early version of what could be defined as a bicycle.

Note the lack of pedals. This *celerifere* from the early 1800s was propelled by the rider's feet.

In the late 1860s, two Frenchmen, engineer Ernest Michaux and mechanic Pierre Lallement, gave the bicycle yet another look with the invention of the *velocipede*. The "bone shaker," as it was informally known, soon evolved into the high-wheeler.

Ernest Michaux with his *velocipede*.

This enormous contraption, consisting of a four foot, six inch front wheel and a 17-inch rear wheel, remains one of the strongest visual images associated with sports of the late 19th century.

The high-wheeler's development coincided with one of the most significant improvements in cycling comfort: the air-filled rubber bicycle tire developed by American John Dunlop in 1868. Engineers discovered that the new rubber tire could be successfully mounted to a thin-spoked wheel. This construction allowed for easier steering and improved both mobility and control.

High Wheeler of 1885

As bicycles became easier to handle, women and children began to ride them, as well. By 1880, cycling was not only the mass transit of choice, but the Number 1 form of family-oriented recreation. This interest created a vigorous business in the production and sale of cycling costumes and accessories similar to today's lively commerce in sports apparel.

Safety bicycle of 1893 with chain-wheel drive.

Soon after the turn of the century, a low-wheeled bicycle—called a safety bicycle—was designed using a chain-wheel drive to the rear axle. It took some time for mechanics to refine this new design and it did not come into popular use until after 1910. But with the invention of the chain-wheel drive, the era of the high-wheeler was over. Since 1900, bicycle design and construction evolved toward the lower, lighter-weight cycles we associate with the modern era.

Racing With the Wind

The 1880s were characterized by unbridled growth in recreational cycling, both in Western Europe and North America. The fun was absolutely contagious; everyone wanted to be outdoors riding. With such enthusiasm in the air, could a match race be far behind? Evidently not, as bicycle racing soon rivaled horse racing as the most popular weekend sport.

By 1885, professional cyclists roamed the countryside putting on exhibitions and challenging locals to a race. To imagine the popularity of their arrival, pretend the Tour de France was to take a side trip through your neighborhood—everyone would be out to see their heroes. And so it was in 1885. Cyclists, then as now, were international superstars and even began to receive corporate sponsorship.

Although cyclists were still a loose-knit group, there were attempts at organization. As a result, a sanctioned event was finally developed and the first official cycling world championship took place in Buffalo, New York, in 1888, eight years before the first modern Olympic Games included cycling on its program.

Men's and women's cycling costumes of the 1870s. Note that the lady is riding side-saddle.

At this time, road racing was the most common form of competition, but because of the poor condition of many roads, cyclists felt that tracks would be easier to negotiate, and racing times would be faster. By the end of the 19th century, there were cycling tracks all over Europe and a few in the United States. After experiments with wood, grit, and shale, cement tracks became the international standard.

In the 1890s, England was the hotbed of world cycling, with more than 700 factories producing 750,000 bicycles a year. But by 1900, the market was saturated and many tracks and plants closed following the downturn in demand. To remedy this decline, the *Union Cycliste International* (UCI) was formed in 1900, and under its leadership, world cycling continued to progress.

Today, new developments in design and technology are occurring in countries throughout the world. As a result, many people assume cycling has always been as popular as it is now; but in truth, cycling, especially in the United States, has gone through some dramatic ups and downs.

Cycling in America

Since its invention in France in 1790, cycling has retained its popularity with Western European nations, but American enthusiasm as been an on-again, off-again affair. In the 1920s, an age of unparalleled prosperity in American history, people cast aside their bicycles to indulge their newest passion, the automobile. During the 1930s, a time often referred to as the Great Depression, economics made bicycle transportation attractive once again. This situation continued through the war years, 1941-1945, when the supply of petroleum products was severely restricted. After World War II, the automobile once again became a major American preoccupation and the bicycle again was cast aside. During the 1950s, however, young people rode bicycles while adults wanted to be seen in their cars because to be seen riding a bike might suggest they couldn't afford a car.

By the late 1960s, Americans' obsession with all things mechanical had begun to wane. People became interested in the environment and many believed that the best way to experience nature was on a bicycle, not in an automobile. By the 1970s, it wasn't only young people who peddled around town; adults by the score were leaving their autos at home and purposefully riding their bikes. They rode them to work, for fun, for exercise, to be with their children, to get outdoors— whenever and wherever they could.

This trend continues today. In fact, the United States Cycling Federation (USCF) reports that in 1980 there were 9,089 USCF members. By February 1996, membership had grown to 50,700 men, women and children, representing all 50 states. No wonder the interest in competitive cycling escalates with each Olympic Games' event—people of all ages are taking a keen interest in Olympic cycling and are rooting enthusiastically for their favorite teams.

Photo courtesy of USOC

The fastest cyclists ride in the lowest, inside lane.

Amateur Cycling Opportunities

Youth

The Lance Armstrong Junior Olympic Race Series for 9-to-18 year olds is designed to increase awareness of cycling and to increase racing opportunities for junior cyclists. In 1995, 33 races were held throughout the United States, with nearly 1,500 athletes competing.

Collegians

The National Collegiate Cycling Association (NCAA) program was developed to meet a growing need for a competitive outlet for students at the collegiate level. Among its greatest successes has been the number of women to whom it has introduced the sport: more women participate in this program than in any other significant U.S. cycling program. The NCAA supports three divisions: road, track and mountain biking, and invites teams assembled through a school's recreation sports or club department to compete. Currently 213 schools are members, more than 2,800 riders are licensed and approximately 140 events receive permits each year.

Men and Women

The Fresca Men's Amateur Point Series was developed to identify elite talent for the U.S. national team and to improve the quality of racing, by providing amateur riders with a highly competitive series of events. Twelve events were held in 1995, with more than 1,600 riders participating.

The Fresca Cup Women's Cycling Series provides highly competitive racing opportunities for women and encourages new cyclists to compete. In 1995, the series encompassed 42 regional and national events, with the

USCF assigning points to each rider and with more than 2,300 women participating.

Masters (After 30)
With more than half of USCF members in the masters category of riders who have reached the age of 30, the USCF has established a number of programs for this group. Masters clinics, which are organized by the USCF's regional road and track coaches, are comprehensive. They instruct athletes on evaluating their individual fitness levels, power output and endurance; identifying their strengths and weaknesses; and formulating personalized training programs. In 1995, 15 clinics were held with more than 300 master riders attending. Masters Regional Championships were held in each USCF region, totaling 12 road events and three track events across the country. Masters National Championships attracted more than 1,900 entries for road events and more than 700 for track events.

Riders With Disabilities
USCF has hosted events for the disabled since 1989, and is a resource for identifying organizations that include athletes with disabilities. USCF's Masters and National Championship programs incorporate three disabled sports organizations; Disabled Sports

USA, United States Association for Blind Athletes and U.S. Cerebral Palsy Athletic Association. USCF also publishes a column for cyclists with disabilities in its monthly newsletter, *Cycling USA.*

Long-Distance Cycling Records

For enthusiasts interested in long-distance cycling, the Ultra-Marathon Cycling Association (UMCA) sanctions events throughout the United States. The following is a partial list of long-distance rides you may find to your liking. For more information on long-distance cycling, including details of how to become a participant, contact the Ultra-Marathon Cycling Association.

- Individual Men's Transcontinental Crossing—
  In 1990, Michael Secrest established a coast-to-coast mark of seven days, 23 hours, and 16 minutes.
- Two-Man Team Transcontinental Crossing—
  In 1987, Lon Haldeman and Pete Penseyres set a time of seven days, 14 hours, and 55 minutes.
- Individual Women's Transcontinental Crossing—
  In 1989, Susan Notorangelo made the trip in nine days, nine hours, and nine minutes.
- Two-Woman Team Transcontinental Crossing—
  In 1984, Estelle Grey and Cheryl Marek set a record of 10 days, 22 hours, and 48 minutes.
- Miami, Florida-to-Atlanta, Georgia, 710 Miles—
  Victor Gallo rode from city hall to city hall in 49 hours, 45 minutes.

- Austin-Houston-Austin, 332 Miles—
  Lynn Schmerhorn made the circuit in 34 hours, 59 minutes.

- Portland, Oregon-to-Salt Lake City, Utah, 785 miles—
  At the age of 52, Ray Youngberg did it handily in 64 hours, 40 minutes.

- Reno, Nevada-to-Tucson, Arizona, 849 Miles—
  Ed Levinson of Oakland, California made short work of the journey in 72 hours, 20 minutes (and that was after he rode his bike from Oakland to Reno, traversing the rugged Sierra Nevada mountain range in the process.)

USA Cycling

USA Cycling is the national governing body for amateur and competitive cycling in the United States, a member of the U.S. Olympic Committee, and recognized by the International Cycling Union as the sole sanctioning body for cycling in the United States. **USA Cycling has the second-largest number of participants in the world after soccer.** USA Cycling is the corporate umbrella for the United States Cycling Federation (USCF), the National Off-Road Bicycle Association (NORBA) and the United States Professional Racing Organization (USPRO). The National Bicycle League joined USA Cycling in December 1996. Headquartered at the U.S. Olympic Training Center in Colorado Springs, Colorado, USA Cycling maintains a significant presence on the local level through its 70,000 members and nearly 2,000 clubs in all 50 states, the District of Columbia and Puerto Rico.

NORBA is the national governing body for the continually growing sport of mountain bike racing, with more than 30,000 member riders. Most significantly, mountain bike racing was recently granted status as an Olympic event and made its debut in Atlanta in 1996.

Collegiate cycling is governed by the NCCA, which brings together more than 200 schools and 3,500 riders to compete for national collegiate titles in both road and track racing.

For more information, contact USA Cycling.

Cycling Associations

USA Cycling
One Olympic Plaza ,
Colorado Springs, CO 80909
(719) 578-4581

International Amateur Cycling Federation
Federal International Amateur de Cyclisme (FIAC)
Via Cassia, 490-00198
Rome, Italy

International Mountain Bicycling Association (IMBA)
P. O. Box 7578,
Boulder, CO 80306
(303) 545-9011

League of American Bicyclists (LAB)
formerly League of American Wheelmen
190 W. Ostend St., Suite 120,
Baltimore, MD 21203-3755

(410) 539-3399

National Collegiate Cycling Association (NCCA)
NCCA National Headquarters
One Olympic Plaza ,
Colorado Springs, CO 80909

(719) 578-4581

National Off-Road Bicycle Association (NORBA)
NORBA National Headquarters
One Olympic Plaza
Colorado Springs, CO 80909

(719) 578-4717

Tandem Club of America (TCA)
220 Vanessa Drive,
Birmingham, AL 35242

(205) 991-7766

Ultra-Marathon Cycling Association (UMCA)
2761 N. Marengo Ave.
Altadena, CA 91001

(818) 794-3119

3

Buying A Bicycle

There are several points to consider before buying a bicycle. Two of the most important are 1) the type of cycling you want to do, and 2) the amount of money you can afford to spend. If your goal is simply to take leisurely rides around your neighborhood, you can probably find a suitable bike for a modest amount of money. In fact, a used bike in good condition may be just what you're looking for. On the other hand, if you are serious about long distance or competitive cycling, a bicycle of that caliber will cost quite a bit more.

If you are not yet sure of your goals, consider buying a modestly priced all-purpose bicycle to get started. Take it on short rides, long rides, and, if you can find them, try some smooth off-road trails. See which you most enjoy, then purchase a good bike especially suited to that purpose. The advantage of this approach is that you don't spend a great deal of money for, say, a touring bike, only to discover that what you really enjoy is off-roading.

Bike Shops

There are many advantages to purchasing a bicycle from a reputable bike shop. Most have well-trained, knowledgeable personnel who will answer your questions and spend the time to make sure you get a bicycle that fits you properly and meets your needs. However, if you do not feel that you are getting good service at a particular shop, try another one. Bicycles are expensive; don't buy anything until you are satisfied and your questions have been answered.

When you are ready to move up to a more sophisticated bike, you may be able to trade in your old bike and apply its value to the purchase price of a new one. Bike shops are more inclined to work a fair deal with you if you purchased your old bike from that store.

Full-service bike shops have repair technicians on hand who are familiar with the bikes sold in that shop and can give your bike the very best care. Also, a professional bicycle technician has access to the proper parts—both for repairs and for upgrades—and can give you sound advice about these matters.

Listen carefully to his or her recommendations.

When you purchase a bike at a bike shop, you will be given a "bill of sale" showing that you lawfully purchased the bike and that you are the legal owner. In the event your bike is stolen, your bill of sale from the bike shop lets the police know that you are indeed the rightful owner. A note of caution is in order here: If you purchase a bike from a private party and the bike was stolen to begin with, that person does not have the legal right to issue you a bill of sale. Bicycle thieves cannot legally transfer ownership. Moreover, if you claim ownership of such a bike, you can be liable for accepting stolen property! You can avoid this aggravation by purchasing your bike from a legitimate, professionally operated bicycle shop.

BMX Bikes

One style of bike that is especially popular with young riders is the BMX. This small, sturdy bike gets its name from cross-country motorcycle racing. Motorcycle racing that takes place on a purpose-built track is called "motocross," abbreviated "MX." Enthusiastic young bicyclists first tried to imitate their motorcycle-riding heroes by putting their street bikes through the same leaps, spins and jumps. Needless to say, the street bikes fell apart. Bicycle manufacturers quickly saw the need for small, lightweight—but very sturdy—bikes that could withstand the stress of imitation motocross stunts. Hence, the BMX evolved. The name BMX, therefore, is a cross between "B" for bicycle and "MX" for motocross. Nowadays, there are many manufacturers, both in Europe and in North America, who produce strong, well-built BMX bikes.

When purchasing a BMX bike, keep the following points in mind:

- BMX bikes are not made with the variety of frame sizes available in other types of bikes. The most popular frame sizes are 12- and 16-inch, but a few manufacturers now make a 20-inch frame to fit older/taller BMX enthusiasts.

- You fit a BMX to your body by raising or lowering the seat. Stand next to the bike in your stocking feet. Keep your feet together. When the seat post is bolted in its mid-position, the top of the bicycle seat should be even with your seat. If the seat post is all the way up or down, try another bike. There are two reasons for this: 1) the seat post is at its weakest when in an extreme position, and 2) you have no where to go with the seat if you experience a growth spurt.

- Considering that BMX bikes have only one gear, you do not have to worry about fitting your hands to shift controls, but you do have to make sure the handlebars are comfortable and properly adjusted. Your bike shop can help you with these and other adjustments.

Mountain Bikes

The mountain bike is much more than a "big brother" of the BMX. Although both are well-suited to off-road cycling, the mountain bike gives the rider a choice of gears, and the larger frame, wheel base, and tires give the mountain bike exceptional versatility.

The most important part of a mountain bike is the frame. Yes, this can be said for all styles of bikes, but mountain bikes really take a beating going cross-country, and cyclists often ride miles from civilization. You simply do not want to have major mechanical breakdowns out on the trail. As discussed earlier, BMX bikes certainly get a workout, but cyclists are usually either on a purpose-built track or relatively close to home. If they need a major repair, they don't have far to walk. Not so with mountain bike enthusiasts—they have been known to ride 50 miles or more into the woods.

A strong, well-built and well-maintained machine is especially important to mountain bike racers who, according to competition rules, must be self-sufficient and make their own repairs. For your own safety, learn basic maintenance before venturing too far afield.

This competition mountain bike has shock-absorbing forks.

When purchasing a mountain bike, keep the following points in mind:

- The *reach*—the distance from the seat to the handlebars—is paramount for comfortable mountain biking. This is not an idle luxury, but a vital part of mountain bike safety. When descending hills or climbing in loose gravel or sand, you'll want to shift your weight over your rear tire while keeping a firm, steady grip on the handlebars. You can't do either effectively if the reach is incorrect. The length of the top tube relative to your body proportions is a very important consideration.

- Do not get a bike that is too big for you. It is a common misconception that one is always better off on a "bigger" machine. Actually, you are in jeopardy on a machine that is too big to handle safely and effectively. Sit on the seat in your stocking feet. Place your heels, not your toes, on the pedals and rotate them backward If you cannot keep you heels in contact with the pedals without rocking from side-to-side, you need to lower the seat. If that doesn't do it, get a smaller bike. This one is too big for you.

For easier mounting and dismounting, some cyclists may prefer the dropped tube model.

- Once you have selected a machine, ask the bike shop technician about handlebar extensions. Most mountain bikes come with relatively straight handlebars that are fine for short rides, but for competitive or long-distance biking, you may find that the curved ones give you added comfort and control.

Cruisers

The simplest of all bikes to operate is the cruiser. With its wide seat and upright handlebars, you really do just sit back and cruise. It is the coaster brake application, however, that makes the cruiser the ultimate easy rider. Push backward on the pedals to stop, push forward on them to go, and sit back and enjoy the ride. If your riding is confined to flat terrain and you don't have to go very far at a stretch, the inexpensive, uncomplicated cruiser may be the bike for you. The heavy frame can take a fair amount of bumps and bangs without noticeable damage, and the cruiser adapts very well to accessories such as baskets, book racks, and saddle bags. One reason is that there is almost nothing—gear shift levers, shock-absorbing forks—with which these items could interfere.

Another benefit of the cruiser is its hardiness. If the thought of bicycle maintenance gives you the shivers, a cruiser is your best bet. As long as you have a clean, dry place to store your bike, a general cleaning and a semi-annual oiling are about all the maintenance a cruiser requires. Put air in the tires once in a while and you're in business.

The 3-Speed
The 3-speed is much lighter weight than the cruiser, making it easier to pedal and to steer. Most 3-speeds also have narrower tires than a heavy-framed cruiser, and all multi-speed bikes have hand brakes to both wheels.

If you plan to ride more than five miles at a stretch and/or if you ride in hilly country, you'll be more comfortable on a multi-speed bike.

The 3-speed has a wider seat and upright handlebars.

Most 3-speed bikes have rather wide seats and upright handlebars, similar to those on a cruiser. If you ride in heavily congested areas where speed is not an issue, the upright position makes it easier for you to see obstacles around you. If you plan to do any long-distance riding or if you must traverse steep hills, you may find a 10-speed more comfortable and easier to ride.

The 10-Speed

For many cycling enthusiasts, the ultimate machine is the sleek-as-a-cat 10-speed road racer. Yes, we realize that *Tour de France* competitors have 16 gears to play with, but we're talking reality here. If you plan to do any racing, long-distance touring or major hill climbing, you'll need a 10-speed. The large wheels fitted with hard, narrow tires eat up the ground as no other machine can. The turned-down handlebars position you in a more horizontal frame, giving you better wind resistance, allowing you the most efficient means of traveling farther and faster.

If you plan to do any long-distance riding, the seat—professionally known as the saddle— will be of paramount importance. You simply cannot be bothered with an irritating, uncomfortable saddle on a long ride. Racing saddles often are made of titanium, but touring saddles are usually made of plastic or high-quality leather. Some long-distance riders favor plastic because it does not absorb moisture and therefore cannot harbor bacteria, but others prefer leather because, being a natural surface, it breathes and conforms slightly to the rider's body. There any many fine saddles on the market and the choice is entirely yours. Be sure to keep leather saddles out of the rain and occasionally wipe them with saddle soap or leather oil (never machine oil) to keep them soft and pliable.

Turned-down handlebars and large wheels embody the most efficient design for long-distance riding.

Bikes with five or more speeds have special gear changers called *derailleurs*. Bikes with derailleurs have one or two gearshift levers. When you move them, the chain moves from one-sized gear to another. A low gear gives the bike the power to climb hills, while a high gear is more efficient on flat, open country.

Whichever bike you choose, give it good care and it will reward you with years of enjoyment.

4

CLOTHING & ACCESSORIES

Perhaps the two most important considerations when selecting clothing and accessories are safety and comfort. By no means is it necessary to wear the latest fashion or the most expensive brand of apparel, but it is worthwhile to invest in a few items. Clothing especially made for cycling is designed to give you a smoother, more comfortable ride.

Helmets
The most essential piece of equipment you will ever buy is your helmet. For riding in sanctioned events, helmets must conform to specific safety standards. Use this standard as a guideline when selecting a helmet, even for recreational riding. Don't waste your money on a flimsy helmet; get one that meets rigid safety standards.

Most employees at top-quality bike shops are very knowledgeable about how cycling helmets should fit. Tell them what type of riding you do and let them guide you in your selection. The three components that make up proper fit are comfort, weight and ventilation.

Photo by Sandra Applegate

A cycling helmet is an essential piece of equipment for riders of every age and skill level.

First, look for a helmet with good ventilation. Openings along the length are best, with additional holes at the sides. This arrangement will give you the best air flow over your head and will carry excess heat away from your skull.

Once you have found a style with good ventilation, choose the correct size. You can ensure a snug fit by using the additional foam pads that come with most helmets. Once the pads have been inserted, adjust the retention straps. These straps keep the helmet in its proper position on your head.

Put on the helmet and secure the straps. Now, shake your head from side-to-side. How does it feel? The helmet should feel snug, yet you should have complete flexibility. Tip your head forward and back. If the helmet is too heavy, the weight of trying to balance it all day will severely tire your neck muscles and quickly lead to fatigue.

Photo by Richard Burns

Full-head helmets are an excellent choice for very young children.

No matter what else you like about it, never buy a helmet that is too heavy for your body.

Next, can you see clearly? The helmet should not impair your vision. If it comes too far forward on your face, it's probably too big for you. Does the helmet work well with your glasses? Try them both on and shake your head. If the glasses slip out of position, something is wrong. Try repositioning the helmet. If that doesn't solve the problem, it may be that the fit of the glasses is not compatible with the outline of that particular helmet. One or the other will have to go.

Finally, can you hear? No helmet should be so bulky around your ears that you cannot hear clearly. If this is a problem, select another style and repeat the process.

Each of the above steps is important in finding and selecting a properly fitting helmet. No step should be overlooked.

Eye Protection
Protective lenses deflect the glare of the sun and protect your eyes from dirt, grit and other intrusions. For casual or recreational riding, you might think a long-billed cap or colored contact lenses are all the protection you need because they can deflect the sun, but they

can't protect your eyes from debris. Dark glasses are helpful on both counts, but the lenses *must* be made of plastic, not glass. Moreover, if you have a fall or other mishap and break your glasses, you might have a hard time seeing until they can be repaired.

Photo by Sandra Applegate

Some goggles are cool!

The best solution is goggles. They fit snugly to keep out wind, dust and other debris; they are made of shatter-proof material; and they can deflect the sun on bright days.

Moreover, the yellow lens actually increase illumination on dark, overcast days.

Gloves

Gloves really do help protect your hands and almost any style of leather or suede gloves is fine for getting started. Gloves with nylon or acrylic palms and fingers should be avoided because they don't provide a secure enough grip on the handlebars or levers. If you really want to be fancy, you can buy a pair of racing gloves, which have gel pads in the palms to improve shock absorption. The casual or

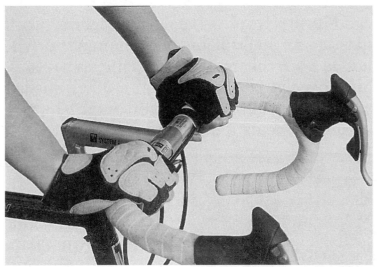

Photo by Sandra Applegate

Cycling gloves have mesh backs for comfort.

recreational rider may not need or want such elaborate accessories. Also, cycling gloves are cut off at the knuckle, thereby exposing your fingers. You may find that regular gloves are more comfortable for you.

Shoes

Although it is not necessary to buy all the bells and whistles for recreational riding, a good pair of cycling shoes is an investment in safety. Sneakers and other types of athletic shoes are too soft for cycling, and many jogging-type shoes are too wide to fit comfortably and safely on the pedals, especially if you are using toe clips or the newer clipless-pedal system. When selecting cycling footwear, keep in mind that you'll need a stiff sole with an upper shoe that will not be adversely affected by scuffs on rocks or branches. For more advanced riding you will probably want to use pedals with toe clips. Cycling shoes are designed to fit neatly into the toe clips; running shoes are too bulky and can actually be dangerous.

Socks should always be worn when cycling. They protect your feet from friction and convey perspiration away from your skin. Natural-fiber materials work best; nylon and other man-made fabrics do not absorb moisture nearly as well. Whichever type of socks you prefer, wear them when trying on shoes.

Coordinating your socks and shoes will help ensure the best fit, and your best performance as a cyclist.

Shorts and Jerseys
You can increase your comfort by wearing well-fitting cycling shorts. This is not a fashion statement; cycling shorts are cut to make riding as comfortable as possible—this means no bulky inseam to chafe and irritate your inner thighs. Moreover, cycling shorts are cut extra long in the leg, low in front to make breathing easier, and high in back to keep your lower back warm and covered as

you lean forward. For added flexibility, most have either an elastic or a drawstring waist.

For casual riding, a regular T-shirt is fine, but for long-distance rides (and certainly for competitive rides), a cycling jersey is what you need. Cycling jerseys are cut long to keep your lower back covered, yet they gently hug your torso to reduce wind resistance. Any cotton or cotton-blend shirt will do nicely for casual riding. But avoid man-made fabrics that neither breathe nor absorb moisture— these fabrics are not suitable for sports. You will be more comfortable in natural fiber clothing.

Cold and Wet Weather Attire

Not all cycling is done in warm weather. If you find yourself riding on a damp, windy or otherwise cold day, a lightweight sweatsuit or jogging suit will be a welcome addition. Make sure your pants legs are snug enough to stay out of the bicycle's moving parts. If necessary, use a pants clip or wrap masking tape around your ankles, putting the excess material on the *outside*. One word of caution: If your sweat-shirt has a drawstring neck or a hood, make sure the string is not so long that it can become tangled in the handlebars or levers. For the same reason, scarfs and mufflers are not recommended for cycling; it's too easy for them to unwind and get caught in the machinery.

There are specialty items for wet-weather riding and competition riders use many of these products with great success. Most beginners will be riding in one general locale so will not need the variety of materials used by international racers. If you like the idea of wet-weather riding, ask your local bike shop to recommend clothing suitable for your geographic area. There are many differences in the clothing available and you'll want to get something conducive to the weather (temperature, humidity, wind-chill factor, etc.) in your area.

If you live in an area with terribly cold winters, you may want to postpone cycling until the warmer months. But if you choose to ride in the cold, follow a few safety tips. If the temperature reaches 32 degrees F. or below, cover your face. Riding at 20 mph, your flesh can freeze within minutes—and you may not even know it has happened until it's too late.

Wear a wool or wool-blend ski mask or balaclava. Wear plastic, not metal, goggles— metal can freeze to your face! Wear full gloves, preferably insulated ones; and keep your body warm. Do not let perspiration build up on your body. If it does, you could freeze. Ask an experienced cyclist how to dress for cold-weather riding, then follow his or her advice. And finally, if you feel apprehensive about the weather, don't ride. Save it for another day.

Bike Bags

Whether you're commuting to work or heading out for a picnic in the park, the time will come when you'll want to carry papers or belongings with you on your ride.

There are many fine bike bags on the market, ranging widely in size, material, and price. Pick one you like. The important point is to select a true bike bag; i.e., a bag specifically made to be attached to a bicycle. Tying your gym bag or lunch sack to the handlebars is very hazardous. These items can shift while you are riding, get caught in the spokes or stuck under the handlebars, and make it impossible to control the bike. This situation is very perilous if you are riding in traffic.

There are two basic styles to choose from: *panniers*, which fit like saddle bags on a horse, and *bags* which attach to the handlebars or seat. Go to your local bike shop and select a bike bag large enough to meet your needs.

If you get a bag that is too small, you'll soon have loose items sticking out the top. This is not good. Get one full-sized bag, or two smaller saddle bags, depending on your needs.

Some of the newer bags have map holders, insulated compartments for food and extra water bottles, internal stiffeners to keep a soft item from being crushed, and detachable shoulder straps so you can carry the bag with you when you're off the bike.

A bike bag is an investment in safety. Select one that fits your needs, your bike, and your price range. You'll be glad you did.

5

CYCLING SAFETY TIPS

When we think of recreational cycling, we may visualize ourselves peddling at a leisurely pace down a quiet country lane, gazing at the trees and flowers along the way. Unfortunately, for an ever-increasing number of cyclists, especially urban dwellers, that scene is simply not a reality. In many parts of the country, the only place cyclists have to ride is on crowded city streets—and that takes special cycling skills.

Riding in Traffic
Do not antagonize drivers of motor vehicles. Even if you believe that you are correct and the driver of the car or truck is in error, your first concern should be for your safety—not your rights. A car or truck is much bigger, heavier, and stronger than your bike. Never

argue. Let them go first or go around you, whatever they want to do. Keep yourself safe.

You can do a lot to ensure your safety by riding in a predictable manner. Motorists will feel more comfortable if they see you riding smoothly in a calm, controlled manner. Swerving and weaving your bike along the roadway is confusing to drivers and may cause them to make an erratic move themselves. Remember, a car is bigger than you are—don't force the issue.

Use hand signals to indicate a change of direction. Motorists will have a better chance of staying out of your way if they know which direction you intend to travel.

Look for streets that have a wide shoulder and avoid the busiest streets whenever you can. If possible, adjust your riding schedule so that you are off the street during the heaviest

Sandra Applegate

This businessman commutes in city traffic.

periods of traffic, usually early in the mornings and evenings.

Wear brightly colored clothes during the day and, if you must ride after dark, wear a white jacket or sweatshirt. At night, white shows up better than any other color. Apply strips of reflector tape to your shoes, pants, and jacket. Make sure your bike has a good reflector and apply strips of reflector tape to your bike, as well. Reflector ankle straps serve a dual purpose since they also keep your pants cuffs clean and out of the bike's chain.

Ride in the same direction as the traffic and stay as far to the right as you can. Watch for potholes, drainage ditches, manhole covers, and other urban hazards. In a pinch, ditch to the right, do not turn out into the flow of traffic unexpectedly.

In congested areas, avoid riding side-by-side with another cyclist. This is very irritating to motorists and may cause them to behave irrationally. Two bikes are difficult for a motorist to pass. The driver may squeeze you and the other cyclists together, causing an accident. For everyone's safety, avoid riding two-or-more abreast on busy city streets.

If you use your bike to carry books, groceries, laundry, sporting equipment or any other items, make sure the load is well-balanced and secured. A load of heavy books, for example, can shift without warning, causing you to lose control of the handlebars. You can help ensure your safety by checking that all loads, no matter how small or how light, are well-secured. On windy days, make sure nothing can blow off your bike or out of your basket. Swirling papers or an airborne jacket can be very startling to passing motorists.

At busy intersections, you may be safer by dismounting and walking your bike across the street. Experienced cyclists may prefer to ride across with the traffic, but children and beginners should stop and walk. Once you are on foot, follow crossing directions given for pedestrians, not vehicles.

Never assume a motorist sees you or your bike; defensive cycling is your best protection. At all times be aware of what vehicles around you are doing, and be prepared to react in any emergency.

Cyclists and the drivers of motor vehicles share public streets, and both have the same rights and responsibilities. Cyclists must obey traffic lights, stop at stop signs, and heed other laws such as riding single file in their lane and giving hand signals when turning. Remember that in any dispute with the operator of a motor vehicle over the right-of-way, you are the vulnerable one. Yield, even if you are right.

Road Hazards

Even if you don't ride in traffic or other congested areas, you can still encounter various types of road hazards. In this section, we'll take a look at common hazards that a cyclist may encounter, even on a quiet country lane. Be alert for dogs. Even the most placid dog can be startled by the sight and sound of a passing bicycle. If you are chased by a dog coming from its own yard, try to sprint past the property. Most dogs won't continue to chase you once you are away from their "territory." If that doesn't work, try using your voice sharply, saying "No!" or "Get Back!" If you have a water bottle handy, you might try to squirt just enough water to startle the dog, allowing yourself time to make an escape. On no account should you try to provoke a dog, nor should you try to retaliate if you are chased. Leave the dog alone and get on up the road. Of course, if you are bitten, call the police immediately. Give a good description of the dog and the location of the attack. You may ask bystanders if they know where the dog lives, but leave any encounters with the owner to the police.

Natural hazards you may encounter include wind, rain, fog, snow, ice, mud and sand. Wind can be hazardous for a number of reasons. A strong wind, especially a cross-wind, can make it difficult to control your bike. Keep both hands on the handlebars at all times and try to maintain a smooth, steady pace. Blowing sand and dust can get into your eyes, obstructing your vision. If possible, get to a safe shelter and wait for the wind to ease before continuing.

If you get caught out in the rain, slow down, take a steady grip on both handlebars, and ride toward your destination using a route familiar to you. On a wet surface, your bike will require a much longer stopping distance, so brake gently and allow plenty of room. Also, tires are likely to slip on a wet surface. A slow, steady pace and gentle braking will give you the best traction.

Fog is especially hazardous for motorists. The best plan is not to ride in fog but, if you must, rely on your hearing as well as your vision to alert you to approaching traffic. Do not assume a motorist sees you. Pull way off the road and wait for any vehicles to pass.

Snow and ice can be very treacherous. Novice cyclists of any age would do well to call for someone to come pick them up. Leave winter-weather riding to experienced cyclists. Mud and sand can surprise you. The road or trail may look perfectly smooth, until suddenly your front tire is sinking like a stone. Don't panic. Take a firm hold on your handlebars, but avoid the "death grip." This is important because if you do fall, you don't want to pull the bike over into your face. Gently, shift your weight rearward to distribute more of it over the rear tire. Get your feet down and walk your bike out of the bog.

When riding on pavement, keep an eye out for oil slicks. These can be very treacherous. Ride around oil slicks whenever possible, but check for traffic first. If you can't ride around it safely, get off and walk.

Potholes, railroad crossings, cattle guards, and drainage grates are all snares waiting to ambush the inattentive cyclist. Railroad tracks, cattle guards, and drainage grates should be crossed at a bit of an angle. This approach keeps your front tire from getting stuck in the cracks. Avoid potholes, especially those filled with water. You can't tell how deep they really are. Heavy jolts are very hard on your bike's suspension. Whenever possible, ride around potholes. Why beat up your bike when you don't have to.

Climbing and descending hills can be loads of fun on a bike, but be aware that your rear tire may slip, especially if you hit loose sand or gravel. When traversing hills, you may want to use a lower gear, or try shifting your weight backward over your rear tire. Both techniques will help you gain better traction.

Sharing Roads and Trails

If you see horseback riders approaching, stop and allow them to pass you. Let them get several yards away before you continue. If you come up behind horseback riders, softly call out and request permission to pass. This gives the riders time to get their horses under control. Meeting horses on the road or the trail is a situation where you really have to use common sense and courtesy. Even if you have the technical right-of-way, it is much easier for you to control your bike than it is for a rider to control a live horse. Realize that horses can become easily frightened by a bicycle. Use your head. Yield the right-of-way to horses and everyone will get where they are going—safely and happily.

Although we do not usually think of horseback riders and joggers as "road hazards"—after all, we all have the right to use the trails—certain conditions involving horses and joggers can be hazardous if not handled properly. If you encounter a jogger, do not assume the person heard you coming and will move out of "your" way. You don't own the road. Pass joggers and hikers carefully, and always leave plenty of room. Joggers, especially, may be very tired, and having to dodge your bike could cause them to stumble and fall. Again, common sense and courtesy represent the best approach.

Theft Prevention
It is a sad statistic, but millions of bicycles are stolen every year. Oddly enough, bicycle owners themselves contribute to that alarming number by leaving their bikes unlocked and unattended. An unlocked bike is an invitation to a bicycle thief. Here are some safety tips from various law enforcement agencies on how you can help protect your bike from thieves.

Tether your bike using a strong chain or steel cable—and buy a good lock. You may have to pay a little more for a quality chain and lock, but think of it as an investment in your bike's security.

Secure your bicycle to an object that cannot be easily moved; a lamppost, tree, or metal bike rack are all good choices. Make sure to keep your bike out of walkways and doors—you have a responsibility to pedestrians to park your bike out of the way.

Take clear, close-up pictures of your bike, at least one shot from each side. Make sure you appear in at least one photo and that your face is recognizable. Keep the photos in a safe place where you can find them quickly and easily. If your bike is stolen, show these photos to the police. Furthermore, when your bike is found, the photos will help substantiate *your* claim of ownership.

Write a description of your bike—color, size, style, make and model, and include any identifying marks such as "zig-zag scratch on left-side handlebar." Sign and date this document, then put it in a safe place. Sometimes these little details are what help you identify your bike out of hundreds of stolen bikes recovered by the police. Again, this type of document can help you prove that you are the rightful owner.

Along with the photos, keep a record of your bike's serial number. This will most likely be found somewhere on the bike's frame. If your bike is stolen, give this number to the police.

In some states, cyclists are required to register their bicycles. Even if your state does not have this requirement, you may want to ask your local police department about voluntary bicycle registration—the quicker the police can access your information, the quicker they can identify your stolen bike.

6

FAMILY CYCLING

Two styles of bicycles that are popular for family outings are the tandem and the trailer. The graceful bicycle built-for-two was first popular in the 1890s, more than 100 years ago. In fact, the tandem may be one of the only bicycle styles that has ever had a song written about it. At the height of the Gay Nineties, song writer Harry Dacre proclaimed his love for his sweetheart in the popular ballad "Daisy," in which the lyric notes how she looked so "sweet" on a bicycle built for two.

Today, tandems are more popular than ever. In fact, since the mid-1980s, the two types of bicycles that have gained most in popularity are the tandem and the mountain bike. Also gaining in popularity is the trailer, especially when fitted with a child's seat.

Tandems
What is it like to ride a tandem? First, tandems require good teamwork and good

communication between the two riders. The person in front is called the "captain," while the person in back is called the "stoker." The origins of these terms have been lost through the years, but they are very appropriate. The captain has control of his or her ship, while the stoker's main job is to provide power to the pedals. There are many benefits that go with being a stoker—he can read maps, give turn signals, and act as a traffic spotter for the captain. Moreover, while the captain is busy watching the road, the stoker can look around and view the scenery.

Courtesy of Tandem Club of America

Modern tandem outfitted with three water bottles for a long-distance ride.

Tandems come in a variety of prices, sizes and styles. For casual riding, you may prefer a mountain bike tandem with straight handlebars and an upright riding position.

For long-distance touring, you may prefer a racing tandem, complete with downturned handlebars, narrower saddles, and more aerodynamic riding positions.

If you want to try a tandem, go to a bicycle store that specializes in tandems. Many bicycle stores can order a tandem for you, but if the store personnel are not familiar with tandems, they may, unknowingly, recommend the wrong cycle for you, or order one that simply will not fit. If your bicycle store is not familiar with tandems, ask if there are any experienced tandem cyclists in town. Check with local bike clubs as well as community recreation departments.

If you find a tandem specialist, pay careful attention to his or her instructions about how to ride a tandem. There are certain techniques that are different from riding a single, and if you learn to use them effectively, your tandem riding will be safer and more enjoyable. For more information, contact the Tandem Club of America.

Trailers

Another variation on family cycling is the child trailer. The best child trailers have a wide wheelbase for stability, thick tires for traction, and a cushioned seat for shock absorption. The mountain bike is strong, stable and has good balance and braking, and many cyclists consider it the ideal choice for towing a trailer.

Children of any age should be outfitted with helmets, and reflector tape should be applied to the rear and both sides of the child trailer. On warm days, a net covering protects children from direct sun. On cool, damp or windy days, a snap-on hood keeps children warm, yet transparent side curtains enable them to see out.

Tandems are far more adaptable than people realize. For example, you can outfit most tandems with a youth seat and raised pedals so that an older child can ride safely, yet have a parent or other adult in the captain's seat to do the steering and braking. For a child just learning about cycling, a tandem or trailer arrangement provides a safe environment for them to learn how to deal with traffic, rules of the road, and other situations.

Racing

In case you still think tandems belong only in Victorian novels, bear in mind that some of the fastest, slickest bicycle racing you'll ever see takes place on modern-day racing tandems. For one thing, the extra weight of two riders, plus double the peddle power, translates into serious speed. Many clubs nationwide hold special tandem races, while others allow tandems to participate in all classes. Hint: Tandems very often win open events because the extra speed gives them enormous advantage. Consider, too, that the stoker has a built-in drafting partner. That situation allows him or her to keep peddling at full power longer than could most solo cyclists.

Courtesy of Tandem Club of America

Successful tandem racing requires split-second timing and communication between the riders.

Tandem racing requires split-second timing and an almost "sixth sense" level of communication between the two riders. Of course, you and your partner must practice at the recreational level before you tackle a race, but the opportunities for tandem cycling are limited only by your imagination. If you have always wanted to cycle, but did not feel up to doing it alone, perhaps a tandem partner is just what you've been waiting for.

Mountain Biking

Mountain biking continues its rise in popularity with 25 million mountain bike riders in 1993. And more than 40,000 newcomers try mountain-bike racing every year.

The National Off–Road Bicycle Association (NORBA), the national governing body for the sport of mountain-bike racing in the United States, sanctions racing and touring events throughout the 50 states and promotes the sport internationally.

For mountain-bike racers, competing with other racers who are at the same skill level is very important. Riders with better skills and more strength can be discouraging opponents for a beginner, while those with fewer skills can impede a skilled rider's development. NORBA classifies its members, first by age level and, second, by ability and racing proficiency.

Class

Junior:	18 and under
Senior:	19–34
Veteran:	35–44
Master:	45 and up

Category

Beginner: For the entry level rider who learns to understand the sport and experience the thrill of mountain biking.

Sport: This category is for riders whose skills, strength, and stamina have improved beyond the beginner level. Most riders in events are in this class.

Expert: For the rider with exceptional skills, strength, and stamina. Very competitive.

Pro: At this level, you are qualified to race internationally as well as locally.

More information on local clubs for this fast–growing sport can be obtained from the NORBA headquarters in Colorado Springs, Colorado.

At the 1996 Olympic Games in Atlanta, Georgia, mountain-bike racing made its debut as an officially sanctioned Olympic event, with both men's and women's cross–country racing. Fifty riders competed in the men's event; 30 riders in the women's. The mountain bike course will not have long climbs, but will have short steep climbs, plus single-track, double-track, and open-jeep trails.

Millions of mountain bike fans watched on July 30, 1996 when their sport was showcased around the world to other enthusiasts.

7

FITNESS & HEALTH

Recreational cyclists do not need a round-the-clock training regime, but even casual riders will benefit from a sensible, effective exercise and physical fitness program. According to many sports experts, the best way to begin any fitness program is *slowly.* Just as you would not try to ride 500 miles your first day out, your off-the-bike fitness program must build gradually, as well. Take it easy and progress slowly, but steadily.

A proper warm-up is essential, and the cornerstone of your fitness program should be the stretching exercises. Cycling keeps muscles, tendons and nerves contracted; your arms, legs and back do not get to operate through their full range of motion. This contracted state is demanding on the body and must be relieved. The best remedy is a total range-of-motion workout—and that means stretching.

Stretching

One way to strengthen and limber your body is to stretch every day, even on the days you do not ride your bike. Do not pull yourself into an exaggerated or painful position—that is not stretching, that is torture. Such extremes will not help you and may even cause an injury. Follow these simple guidelines for effective stretching.

If you are warming up out-of-doors, stay out of drafts and keep your body warm. A light-weight sweatsuit is ideal, and you can easily put it on over your cycling clothes. After you warm up, keep the suit on until you are ready to ride. Drink fluids to cool and refresh your body, but do not expose yourself to a blast of cold air.

If you are stretching indoors, find a spot with plenty of open space. Your efforts will be pointless if the space you are working in is so cramped you cannot extend yourself. When stretching indoors be mindful of air conditioning. The effect can be as deleterious as any out-of-doors elements. Keep your body warm and protected.

Once you have found a comfortable place to exercise, clear your mind of any stress and relax. It is hard to get the benefit of your stretching exercises if your mind remains cramped. Your goal is to loosen and limber your body, and it is hard to do that unless your mind is equally relaxed.

Start slowly. Affect an easy stretch and hold that position for 20 to 30 seconds. Release slowly and repeat on the opposite side of your body. For example, if you begin by stretching your left arm, repeat that exercise with the right arm. Stretch and hold both sides of your body for the same length of time.

Never bounce. Years ago people thought bouncing helped stretch the muscles. Fitness experts now know this is not true. Bouncing is, in fact, counterproductive. It tightens the very muscles and ligaments you are trying to stretch.

Resist any temptation to rush through your exercises. Take your time, breath slowly and deeply, concentrate on what you are doing. Relax.

It is natural to feel a little tighter or stiffer on some days than on others. Do not force the issue and do not hurt yourself by trying to "work it out." Your body is telling you it is tired—give it a rest. Do a light workout and leave the more difficult moves for another day.

The following stretches will help you avoid most of the physical problems encountered by cyclists. Note: If this is a cycling day for you, take a leisurely ride on flat ground. Tackle the hills on a day when you feel more limber.

Neck Stretches

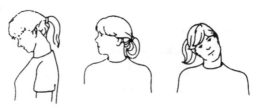

Illustrations in this chapter courtesy of USA Cycling

Stretch your neck in three steps. First, tilt your head repeatedly from front to back. Then, tilt it from side to side. Finally, rotate it in a circular motion.

Shoulder Stretch

Stretch your arms both down to your waist and then behind your head, an arm at a time. Rotate your arm in each position to make sure that all of your shoulder muscles are stretched.

Quadriceps Stretches
While leaning on a solid object, grab your ankle and pull it upward with your arm. Alternate legs.

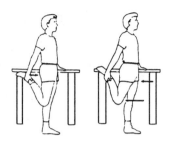

Calf Stretch
With your weight on the front foot, bend your rear knee forward to stretch your calves and your achilles tendons. Be sure that the toes of the rear foot remain on the ground. Then, alternate legs.

Hamstring Stretch

Perform this stretch by flattening your back and leaning forward. This stretches the extended leg. Alternate legs.

Lower Back Stretch

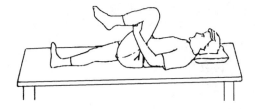

While lying on your back, alternately pull each knee toward your chest and slowly straighten your leg.

Wrist Stretches

With your fingers pointing toward your knees, lean forward. This stretch helps prevent handlebar palsy.

Remember that regular stretching is the key to success. A light session every day is far more beneficial (and healthier) than one rigorous session once in a blue moon.

Toning and Conditioning

Many cyclists like to augment their bike riding with regular workouts at a gym. One advantage of a good gym or health club is the access it gives you to resistance training (also known as weight training) machines.

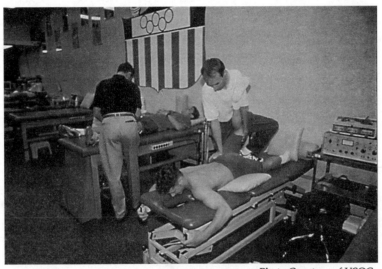

Photo Courtesy of USOC

A good rub-down relaxes and tones muscles and ligaments, and is an essential training component for all U.S. Olympic and elite athletes. Many gyms and fitness centers now offer massage therapy. If possible, make massage a part of your overall conditioning program.

Many sports experts who specialize in cycling recommend the use of machines rather than free weights. It is too easy to hurt yourself waving free weights around in all directions. The machines give you a controlled workout.

Start with the lowest weight setting and increase the amount of resistance a little at a time. For optimum health and fitness, stretch before and after working on the machines.

Saddle Sores

Frequently, riders develop saddle sores during the conditioning phase of training. The reason is that you are now spending more time on your bike and taking a little more serious approach to your riding. The increase in stress, training, and time in the saddle all contribute to the development of skin rashes, saddle sores and other discomforts.

The good news is that, if treated immediately, most saddle sores disappear within a few days and do not cause lasting or serious damage. The operative phrase here is "if treated immediately." Never leave a saddle sore, or any other skin irritation, untreated.

The term "saddle sore" is actually a collective term for any skin irritation, pain, or abrasion, around your crotch, seat bones or inner thigh area. Those parts of your skin that rest on or rub against the bicycle seat are subject to chafing and other problems. Saddle sores are most often caused by one of three situations: friction, pressure, or infection.

Chafing of the inner thighs is a very common friction-induced condition. When the inner thighs repeatedly rub against the sides of the bicycle seat—a condition that occurs during pedaling—the skin becomes raw and irritated. Left untreated, chafing can become very severe. The best approach is to wash and gently dry the legs every day, exposing them to fresh air and as much sunlight as possible. Some people find relief with topical creams and lotions, others like to use dry powder. All of these are fine and largely a matter of choice, but the most important step is good daily hygiene.

Saddle sores are often caused by pressure on the crotch and inner-thigh area. As your training and conditioning increase, you will naturally be spending more time on your bike, riding more miles per session. Pressure can build during long rides, preventing small blood vessels from bringing a full supply of blood to the skin. When the skin gets a less-than-adequate blood supply, saddle sores can quickly develop. If you begin to feel discomfort, get off your bike and walk around for a few minutes. Walking will restore an adequate blood supply to your body, and give cramped muscles and nerves a chance to stretch and open up, as well.

As soon as you get home, remove your cycling clothes and get right into a shower or bath. Dry thoroughly and, if possible, wear loose-fitting clothing for the remainder of the day. Unrestrictive clothing will allow your body to get the fresh air it needs. Fresh air to the skin reduces the chance of developing an infection.

Infection can be controlled by keeping yourself and your clothes clean and fresh. For long-distance riding, it is best to wear padded cycling shorts designed to whisk moisture away from your body. Avoid wearing the same shorts two days in a row without first laundering them and letting them dry completely. Worn clothing holds bacteria and increases your chances of developing a skin infection.

If you do not have or cannot afford more than one pair of "real" cycling shorts, that's fine. Simply wear sweatpants or another pair of comfortable shorts, preferably cotton, on alternate days. Jerseys, T-shirts and socks likewise should be changed daily. A sweaty T-shirt or dirty socks invite bacteria.

Pay special attention to your feet, especially the tender skin between your toes. This is an area where bacteria love to hang out, causing the painful disease commonly known as "athlete's foot." You can usually beat this monster by keeping your feet clean and allowing them to dry thoroughly after every washing, and by wearing clean socks every day. Taking care of your cycling clothes is not about making a fashion statement, it is about protecting your health.

Nutrition

Your diet is an important part of your overall physical fitness. Basically, food consists of three categories: carbohydrates, fats and protein. All are vital for good health, but athletes most often focus on carbohydrates. This is because carbohydrates are the primary source of fuel and with the demands that athletic endeavors put on the body, a steady supply of carbohydrates is essential.

Carbohydrates come in two forms: complex (starches) and simple (sugars). The most nutritious are the complex carbohydrates found in foods such as potatoes, bread, pasta, lentils, vegetables and nuts. In addition to the necessary starch found in these foods, they also provide all the vitamins and minerals necessary to metabolize (break down) the carbohydrates. The assimilation process is essential if the body is to utilize the nutrients found in the foods. Without it, the nutrients pass right through the body, giving little or no benefit.

Carbohydrate-rich drinks are an effective way of replenishing the nutrients your body needs during vigorous exercise such as cycling. You can prepare a healthful drink and carry it on your bike in your water bottle. A complex carbohydrate drink prepared by mixing corn starch with water is very nutritious. The corn starch is flavorless and the drink contains no salts or sugars to cause an upset stomach. If you don't want to mix your own, there are many commercially prepared drinks available. By sipping at regular intervals, you can rehydrate and feed your body at the same time.

Simple carbohydrates, found in confectionery, processed foods and soft drinks, provide quick energy, but offer no lasting benefits. Consumption of these foods and drinks should be kept to a minimum.

Few people in the western world need to fear not getting enough fat in their diet. On the whole, we should reduce the amount of fat we ingest rather than concern ourselves with how to ingest more. Some fat, of course, is essential for good health, but the amount of fat in the average diet is already excessive. Fat does have some benefits. It is an insulator in cold weather and provides a long-range source of energy, but unless you are cycling a very long distance, your source of fuel should be carbohydrates, not fat.

Protein is the athlete's friend. Among its many functions, protein builds and repairs muscle tissue—and every athlete wants and needs strong, healthy muscles. The best sources of protein are white meat, fish, beans, legumes, nuts and milk.

In addition to carbohydrates, fats, and proteins, a cyclist should not overlook the importance of water. Sixty percent of your body weight is water, and you need it to lubricate your joints and maintain your body's temperature. Water also transports the nutrients you need to stay healthy. No one's body ever adapts to dehydration, so the cyclist must stay hydrated by drinking water. Do not let yourself become thirsty. If you do, you've waited too long to rehydrate.

A final caution: Avoid alcohol and the caffeine drinks—cola, coffee, and tea. They are diuretics that drain your body of fluids.

It is important to fuel your body before you embark on a long ride but to avoid excess fat and any foods difficult to digest. After all, the purpose of your meal is to give you energy, not a stomachache.

While there are no "miracle" foods, by eating a carbohydrate-rich diet the cyclist can improve performance and extend endurance for those long rides. The Cycling Federation's suggested diet plan is as follows:

A few days before a ride: Eat 600 grams of carbohydrate per day and drink at least eight glasses of pure water.

Three hours before a ride: Eat one solid meal that you would normally eat every day.

Two hours before a ride: Hydrate your body by drinking one liter of water or a sports drink.

Ten minutes before a ride: Drink one bottle of pure water.

During your ride: After 15 or 20 minutes, begin drinking a high–carbohydrate sports drink. If this is a long ride of more than three hours, have bagels or other high–carbohydrate foods, and a sports drink with a 5 to 10 percent carbohydrate concentration. Keep in mind that you want to replace the fluids your body will lose while you are riding.

Experiment with different foods during training, but never during a race.

Finally, eat before you are hungry, and drink before you are thirsty!

If you have additional questions about good food choices for cyclists, consult your doctor. You may also find helpful information by contacting the sports medicine departments of various universities.

8

First Aid & Safety

Although bicycle riding is not considered a contact sport, an accident or injury can happen to anyone at any time. In cycling, the two most common mishaps are falls and collisions. Fortunately, most spills are not serious, yet never take a chance with an injured person. The following guidelines will help everyone optimally cope with an injured rider.

- **Remain Calm.** The injured cyclist's recovery may depend on the decisions you make, and it's hard to make accurate decisions when you're flustered. Moreover, your behavior may determine the reactions of others around you, including cyclists, parents, and spectators, and no one will benefit from extreme or hysterical reactions when level-headed judgment is called for.

- **Stay In Control.** Resist the urge to move an injured cyclist to a more comfortable location (such as under a shade tree). Only if the cyclist is in imminent danger should he or she be moved. Whenever there is any doubt as to the nature or extent of an injury, call for emergency assistance (fire, police, etc.). You may cover the injured person with a blanket or jacket to keep them warm and reduce the chance of shock, but let them stay where they are until help arrives.

- **Move Bicycle.** For safety reasons, it may be necessary in some cases to move fallen bicycles out of the path of oncoming traffic. Another option would be to flag oncoming traffic and route it around the accident site. In either case, be extremely careful—never put yourself or another person in danger by trying to salvage a fallen bike. Bicycles, no matter how fancy, can be replaced. Let the bike go; safety is your primary consideration.

The First Aid Kit

It is a good idea to keep a basic first aid kit on hand at all times. Many pharmacies and sporting goods stores carry well-stocked first aid kits, but if you want to put one together yourself, the following items should be included:

- Adhesive bandages of various sizes
- Antiseptic soap (for washing a wounded area)
- Antiseptic solution (for bug bites, minor scrapes)
- Aspirin
- Blanket to cover injured cyclist (warmth reduces chance of shock)
- Cold packs
- Elastic bandages (various sizes)
- Eyewash solution
- Gauze pads (various sizes)
- Hank's solution (trade name Save-a-Tooth)

- Sterile cotton sheets (can be cut to fit)
- Scissors
- Tissues and pre-moistened towelettes
- Tweezers (for splinters)
- Small utility knife; *e.g.*, a Swiss Army knife for use on trail rides

The phone number of the nearest ambulance service should be taped to the inside of the first aid kit. If you ride as a club or group, all cyclists should know where the first aid kit is stored, and where it will be kept at races and other events. The best first aid kit in the world does you no good if you can't find it when you need it. When riding at sanctioned events, make sure someone in your group knows the location of the closest telephone; and always keep a quarter or two in the kit so you won't have to hunt for change in an emergency.

Treating Road Burns

Learning proper bike-handling skills will help reduce your chances of falling, but even the best cyclists fall occasionally. If you or someone in your cycling group falls, the following information will help you treat skin abrasions commonly known to cyclists as "road burns."

Road burns are graded by level of severity, similar to the grading system used for other types of burns: first, second and third degree.

First degree applies when there is only a reddening of skin. In a first-degree burn, the skin is not broken and there is no bleeding. Generally, these are minor wounds and can be treated by washing the bruised area with clean, cool water and a mild antiseptic soap. If necessary, an ice bag may be applied for a few minutes to help reduce discomfort and take away any stinging sensation.

Second-degree burns are more serious. In this case, the injured person suffers reddening, broken skin and bleeding. Frightening as it sounds—and, no doubt, looks at the time—most second-degree road burns heal beautifully and, believe it or not, rather quickly. Proper emergency treatment of the injured party promotes successful healing .

Keep the injured person quiet, preferably in a sitting or lying-down position. This helps to reduce shock and keeps an adequate supply of blood flowing to the brain. In cases of severe bleeding, your first concern should be to staunch the flow. Bind the wound and keep it bound. In any injury where there is excessive bleeding, do not worry about cleaning the wound. Your efforts should be directed toward stopping the bleeding and getting a doctor or rescue team to the injured person.

In cases of minor bleeding, you may attempt to clean the wound before bandaging it. Pour a bit of the antiseptic soap onto a wad of sterile cotton. Gently clean the wounded area of any surface debris, but leave deep probing to a qualified physician. To control bleeding and keep wounds clean, place a non-stick gauze pad over the abrasion. Cover that with a fresh cotton sheet, then bind the wound with an elastic wrap. Do not make your wrap too tight. For wounds covering a smaller area, repeat the cleaning procedure described above, but cover the wound with an adhesive bandage, cut it to fit if necessary.

If the injured person remains conscious, give them fresh, cool water to drink. Fresh water flowing through the system helps the lymph glands carry away any infectious bacteria. If the injured person is unconscious or drifts in and out of consciousness, refrain from giving them anything to eat or drink. They could easily choke, causing even more serious problems.

The injured person should be taken to a doctor for follow-up treatment as soon as possible. Extensive cleaning or suturing should be attempted only by a qualified physician. Once a second-degree wound begins to heal, the fresh, tender skin must be protected from the sun. Young skin does not have the inner-protective capabilities of older skin and must be protected from harmful ultraviolet rays.

Third-degree burns are the most serious. In this type of burn, the skin has been entirely removed, possibly exposing underlying layers of muscle and/or bone. An injury of this type demands immediate professional care. Do not move the injured person. Get a doctor or rescue team to them, post haste. Fortunately, most cycling falls are not this severe. We mention it here only so you will have an idea of the degrees of injury possible, and an understanding of how best to handle each situation. Stay calm, think, and do the best you can under the circumstances. When in the slightest doubt, call for emergency assistance. This is the smartest call you can possibly make.

Handling a Dislodged Tooth

Most times when a tooth has been knocked out it can be replanted and retained for life, especially if the tooth has been properly handled. One critical factor determining a successful replant is the care and handling of a dislodged tooth.

The best way to store a tooth is to immerse it in a pH-balanced, buffered, cell-preserving solution such as Hank's or Viaspan® (used for transplant organ storage). Hank's solution (under the trade name Save-a-Tooth) may be purchased over-the-counter at many drug stores. It will store the tooth in a safe container for 24 hours and has a shelf life of two years. With the use of a proper storage and transport container, there is an excellent chance of having a dislodged tooth successfully replanted.

Vision and Corrective Lenses

Your vision, just like the strength in your arms and legs, is an important part of your overall performance. The demands on your visual system during sporting activities are rigorous. To ride your best, you must know what is behind you, beside you, and in front of you at all times, and this takes a variety of vision skills. If your natural vision affects your athletic performance, ask your doctor about glasses or contact lenses.

Today's eye-care specialists use a wide variety of lens materials. One such development is the new impact-resistant lens now available for use in prescription glasses. These lenses are attractive, affordable, lightweight, and will not shatter if broken.

Another option is contact lenses. Available in hard and soft lens materials, contacts offer many excellent advantages to the athlete. For best results, tell your doctor about the type of cycling that you do. That information will be helpful to the doctor in selecting the best lenses for you. If you wear contact lenses, take your cleaning and wetting solutions with you to all cycling events, and notify your coach that you are wearing contacts.

Getting a foreign object in the eye is the most common eye problem associated with cycling. Fortunately, these foreign objects are usually in the form of minor irritants such as dust, dirt, or sand. Goggles will help protect your eyes, especially on windy days. Your local bicycle shop will have many styles to choose from—select one that fits securely and allows a wide field of vision.

Care of the Eyes

More serious injuries, such as a blow to the head, may produce bleeding in or under the skin near the eye, causing a "black eye." An ice pack will reduce swelling until a doctor can evaluate the injury.

Fortunately, the eye has a number of natural defenses. It is recessed in a bony socket and the quick-blinking reflexes of the eyelids and eyelashes deflect most foreign particles. Also, natural tears wash away most minor irritants. If you *do* get something in your eye, follow these simple guidelines:

- Do not rub your eye or use a dirty cloth or finger to remove the obstruction.

- Irritants can often be eliminated by looking down and pulling the eyelid forward and down. Make sure your hands are clean.

- If you see a particle floating on your eye, gently remove it with a clean, sterile cloth or apply an eye wash to flush the obstruction.

Whatever you do for recreation, your vision plays a vital role in helping you enjoy the sport and perform at your best. Your eyes deserve the best of care.

Wrist and Hand Injuries

Injuries to the wrists and hands are most often related to falling, although fingers can be "jammed" during a collision. To reduce the possibility of wrist and hand injuries, follow these simple guidelines:

- Prior to riding, remove all cosmetic jewelry. If you wear a medical-alert bracelet, continue to wear it while cycling, but make sure it is snug enough not to catch on handlebars or brake and shift levers.

- Avoid riding with your fingers straight out. Keep your fingertips and knuckles curled back toward your palms, and keep your thumbs resting alongside your index fingers.

- Avoid putting a "death grip" on your handlebars. Hold your bike firmly, but allow some flex into your elbows and shoulders. This will help prevent stress and muscle fatigue from settling in your hands, thereby reducing your chances of wrist and hand injuries.

- Gloves are a good way to protect your hands. If you fall, gloves keep your hands from getting scratched; and while you ride, gloves protect your hands from friction on the handlebars and from the elements, especially the sun.

Transporting Tips

To be on the safe side, cyclists who have suffered an upper extremity injury should be evaluated by a doctor. To safely transport a person with an arm, wrist or hand injury, follow these steps:

- A finger with mild swelling can be gently taped to an adjacent finger.
- An elastic bandage may be gently wrapped around an injured wrist to give the wrist support. Do not wrap heavily and do not pull the bandage tightly.
- If possible, place a pillow in the rider's lap and allow him or her to rest the injured hand on the pillow. Do not bunch the pillow around the injury.

Ice and Heat Treatments

If a cyclist is injured, elevate the injury (if possible) and apply an ice pack. Use ice instead of heat because coldness reduces both swelling and pain. Leave the ice pack on until it becomes uncomfortable. Allow the injured person to rest for 15 minutes, then reapply the ice pack. Repeat this procedure until any swelling abates or, in more serious cases, until professional medical help arrives.

R–I–C–E (rest, ice, compression, and elevation) is the recommended way to manage an injury and is about all you should do in the way of self–treatment. R–I–C–E reduces the swelling of most cycling injuries and speeds recovery. Two to three 20–minute sessions per day at 90-minute intervals should provide noticeable improvement. Do not overdo it; 20 minutes is long enough.

Naturally, if the injury is severe and there is an obvious deformity, seek professional help as soon as possible.

In most cases, after two or three days or when the swelling has stopped, heat can be applied in the form of warm-water soaks. Fifteen minutes of warm soaking, along with a gradual return to motion, will speed the healing process. Seek the advice of a sports-medicine professional prior to starting your own treatment plan.

Guidelines for Reducing Injuries
Although no amount of planning and preparation can guarantee that a cyclist will never fall or be injured, there are many things

that can be done to reduce the possibility of injury.

Inspect your bike and equipment daily. If you spot a developing problem, take care of it immediately. Do not ride with faulty equipment, no matter how minor it may seem. Get it fixed.

Avoid riding alone, especially on unknown or hazardous trails. Always tell a reliable person where you are going and what time to expect you back. Then keep to that schedule. Ride with a buddy whenever possible.

Novices of any age should avoid riding after dark. Experienced riders should wear reflective clothing and attach reflective pads to their helmets and shoes. Keep headlamp and reflectors clean and in good repair. Most nighttime collisions are the direct result of drivers not being able to see the rider.

Even during the day it is beneficial to wear clothing that allows drivers to see you, as far ahead as possible. Bright fluorescent colors work best.

Always wear a safety helmet and proper footwear. There are many good cycling shoes to choose from, but even a good sturdy pair of sneakers is better than going barefoot.

If you like to ride on a motocross-type course, check the course for hazards *before* you ride. Debris should always be cleared away and dangerous obstacles such as large boulders should be removed or at least flagged.

Take water with you on the trail, and always have a supply of fresh water at every cycling event.

Warm up and stretch before you ride. If the weather is breezy or cold, keep your body covered and avoid drafts. A proper warm-up routine will reduce the possibility of a pulled muscle or other injury. When you return from riding, get out of your cycling clothes as soon as possible. Damp, sweaty clothes increase the chance of muscle stiffness and skin irritation. Shower and dress warmly and as quickly as you can.

Always seek prompt medical attention for an injured person. If you do not know what to do, call for emergency assistance. Do not move an injured cyclist unless he or she is in immediate danger at that location. If you will have to wait long for assistance, cover the injured person with a lightweight blanket. Warmth reduces the chance of shock.

9

BICYCLE MAINTENANCE

No matter what type of bicycle you have, you need to take proper care of it. There are many simple maintenance tasks you can perform yourself to prolong both the life and appearance of your bike.

Cleaning

Check your bike after every ride. If you are lucky enough to have a hanging rack, lift your bike onto the rack before you begin the cleaning process. If you do not have a hanging rack, simply park your bike in a clean, dust-free area before you begin cleaning up. Finding a clean environment is important because dust and sand can blow onto the freshly-oiled parts of your bike, creating a sticky mess.

If the bike has gotten very muddy, you may wish to squirt it off with a hose before beginning your cleaning routine. Do not drown the bike. Just get the mud off, then bring it into the garage or work shed for a thorough cleaning.

Dip a sponge into a bucket of warm, soapy water and give the bike a good wiping down. Use a mild laundry soap or car washing soap; never use anything abrasive. Don't forget to clean those hard-to-reach places. For those particularly difficult areas, you can also use any of several commercial degreasers.

Once you have given it a good washing, go over it lightly with a clean, damp sponge to pick up all traces of soap. Immediately go over the entire bike with a dry turkish or terry-cloth towel. Do not let water dry on the bike itself. You will probably need more than one towel to do the job right. If one towel gets wet, use another. The important thing is to wipe the bike dry.

An old toothbrush works very well for cleaning the chain. Check the chain for wear and adjustment. If it needs to be tightened, do so. Riding with a floppy chain not only is dangerous, it puts wear and tear on other moving parts. Keep the chain clean and the tension properly adjusted.

Once the bike is clean, it is time to oil and grease moving parts. Use bicycle oil, not household oil. You can get bicycle oil at your local bike shop. The chain, gears and brake calipers all need oil. Tire hubs, nuts and bolts need clean, dust-free bearing grease. If you only have oil, use it. The important thing is to keep moving parts lubricated.

Use a stiff brush to remove tiny stones and pieces of glass from front and rear tires. Check them carefully for foreign particles and listen for slow air leaks. If you hear a leak, repair the tire before riding again. Use a tire gauge to determine tire pressure. If one or both tires are low, inflate them to the recommended pressure before riding again. Maintaining proper tire pressure will help prolong the life of your tires and make your rides smoother and more enjoyable.

Give the bike a final inspection. Check brake cables for proper tension. Check handlebar grips for cracks, tears or debris. If the damage is extensive, replace them before you injure your hands. Check your seat for wear and tear, and if the damage is extensive, replace your seat, too. You do not want to be out on a long ride and have your seat start giving you trouble.

Storage

Cleaning is important, but so is storage. Here are some tips to make bicycle storage safer and more convenient.

- Keep your bike protected from the weather, especially rain and hot sun. The damage from rain is obvious, but did you know that direct sunlight is just as damaging? Sun rots your tires and cables, and dries out areas that should be kept lubricated.

- Store your bike in an area where it won't be in anyone's way. It's not fair that passers-by should have to dodge your bike to get in and out of a door. Be polite and keep your bike out of aisle ways and off sidewalks and paths. Also, if your bike is out of the way, it's less likely to be knocked over.

- Keep your bike locked and tethered to a strong, immovable post. For more information about theft prevention, refer to Chapter 5, "Cycling Safety Tips."

- Finally, if you are not going to ride your bike for more than a month, devise some way to hang it by its frame. It's not good for the tires to have to support all of the bike's weight on one small area.

The longer you have your bike, the more you will get to know it. You will be able to feel when something is not right. Knowing your bicycle well means you will know to take it to a reputable bike shop before major damage can occur. Read as much as you can about bicycle repair and ask questions of experts. The more you know about your bicycle, the better you will be at repairing and maintaining it yourself.

10

GLOSSARY

Aerobic—A physical condition in which all the body parts are working to maximum effectiveness.

Attack—An aggressive, high-speed move away from other riders.

Blocking—Legally impeding the progress of riders in the pack to allow teammates a better chance for success.

Breakaway—A rider or group of riders who have outrun the pack.

Bridge—To escape one group of riders and join another group farther ahead.

Butted Tube—A type of tubing found in expensive bike frames. The metal is very thin throughout except at each end, where it thickens to provide strength at tube intersections.

Chase—Riding to catch a breakaway.

Calipers—Bicycle brakes actuated by hand levers.

Categories—The division of USA Cycling classes into smaller groups, based on riding ability and experience.

Century—A 100-mile race.

Circuit—A multi-lap event on a course that usually is two miles or more in length.

Cleat—A metal or plastic fitting on the sole of a cycling shoe.

Clinchers—Conventional tire with a separate inner tube.

Criterium—A mass-start race covering numerous laps of a course that is usually one mile or less in length.

Derailleur—The mechanism that moves the chain from gear to gear.

Downstroke—The time when a rider's foot is pushing down on a pedal; the moment the greatest amount of energy is displaced to the pedal.

Drafting—Riding in the *slipstream* (see Slipstream defined below) of the rider ahead. Drafting cuts wind resistance and saves a great deal of energy.

Dropped Out—A rider who has fallen behind his group.

Echelon—When a crosswind is blowing, each rider positions himself to the side of and slightly behind the rider immediately in front. If the wind is coming from the right, the line of riders will angle off to the left side of the person in front, thereby lessening the negative effect of the wind.

Fat Tire—A common term for the mountain bike and everything that has to do with it.

Feed Zone—A designated area along a race course where support crews may hand food and drink to racers.

Field—The main group of riders. Also known as the "pack," "bunch," or "peloton."

Field Sprint—A dash to the finish line by the largest group of riders remaining in a race; usually, but not always, a pack toward the front.

Forcing the Pace—To increase the pace of a ride to the point that other riders have trouble maintaining the speed and begin to flounder. This tactic works well in racing, but should be avoided on pleasure rides.

Gap—The distance between the leaders and the field, measured in time.

Gnarly—A mountain bike term that denotes admiration and toughness when applied to a person; when applied to a terrain, a way to say "scary" without sounding chicken.

Granny Gear—The lowest gear on a mountain bike.

Hammering—Riding hard; going all out.

Hanging on—Barely maintaining contact at the back of the pack.

Hook—A situation in which two riders collide by locking handlebars or wheels together. To avoid a hook, pleasure riders should allow at least a full arm's length side-to-side and a bicycle length front-to-back.

Hover—In mountain biking, to adjust your weight by lifting your rear end out of the saddle. Relieves your weight only long enough to go over a bump.

Jerk—Mountain bike word for any rider in the vicinity of an accident.

Jump—Any quick, aggressive acceleration. A move frequently used when making an *attack* (see Glossary term Attack).

LAB—League of American Bicyclists. Founded in 1880 as the League of American Wheelmen, this is the oldest organized body of cyclists in the U.S. Among other activities, this politically active group initiates and supports legislation beneficial to cyclists.

Lead Out—A race tactic in which a rider accelerates to his maximum speed for the benefit of a teammate behind him. The second rider then leaves the *slipstream* (see Slipstream) and sprints past the leader at even greater speed. This move is usually executed near the finish line.

LSD—Long, steady distance. A training technique that calls for continuous rides of at least two hours, done entirely at an *aerobic* (see Aerobic) pace.

Lugs—Metal fittings at the intersections of tubes in a frame.

Madison—A pairs track race in which teammates relay one another into contention.

Mass Start—Events in which all contestants leave the starting line at the same time.

Minuteman—In a *time trial* (see Time Trial), the minuteman is the rider who leaves the starting line one place in front of you. So named because in most time trials, riders leave at one-minute intervals.

Mixte—A frame design which has two straight tubes going from the head tube to the rear stay ends, both being attached to the seat tube. This configuration produces a stronger frame than the traditional dropped or scooped-frame construction.

Pace Line—A single-file formation in which each rider takes a turn at the front, breaking the wind for the group before pulling off and dropping to the rear of the pack.

Panniers—Large saddle bags used by touring and recreational riders. These come in pairs and are mounted on a rack that allows them to hang along each side of the rear wheel. Panniers over the front wheel are seen less frequently.

Potato Chip—A wrenched wheel on a mountain bike.

Power Train—The components directly involved with making the rear wheel turn.

Prime—Pronounced *preem*, this is a sprint within a race. Riders who successfully execute this move can earn extra points or prizes.

PSI—Pounds per square inch.

Pull—To ride at the front of a pack.

Pull Off—Move to the side after leading so that another rider can come to the front.

R–I–C–E—An acronym for rest, ice, compression, and elevation. The formula for immediate management of an injury.

Road Race—A mass-start race that goes from one point to another point, covers one large loop, or is held on a circuit longer than those used for criteriums.

Saddle—A bicycle seat.

Saddle Sores—Chafing between the legs. These abrasions must be tended to right away or they can lead to serious problems.

SAG Wagon—A support vehicle that follows a group of riders. Its purpose is to carry equipment and lend assistance where needed.

Single Track—Path or trail only wide enough for one mountain bike rider at a time.

Sit On A Wheel—To ride directly behind someone, thereby receiving benefit of the *draft* (see Slipstream).

Slingshot—A move to sprint around another rider at top speed after drafting.

Slipstream—The area of low air resistance behind a moving cyclist.

Snakebite—A double puncture in a tire that looks like two fang holes. This is the most common flat tire encountered by mountain bikers.

Soft Pedal—To rotate the pedals without actually applying power.

Sprint—A short acceleration to maximum speed.

Sprinter—A rider who excels in short power bursts.

Stage Race—A multi-day event consisting of point-to-point and circuit road races, time trials, and criteriums. The winner is the rider with the lowest elapsed time for all stages.

Team Time Trial—A race against the clock with two or more riders forming a team and working together.

Throw the Bike—A racing technique in which a rider will push the bike as far ahead of his or her body as possible without losing control, thereby hoping to cross the finish line ahead of a competitor.

Time Trial—A race against the clock in which individual riders start at set intervals and cannot give aid or receive it from others on the course.

Trackstand—Balancing in place on the track or at a stoplight.

Tubular—A lightweight racing tire that has the tube permanently sewn inside the casing. The tire is glued onto the rim.

Turnaround—The point where cyclists reverse direction on an out-and-back time-trial course.

USA Cycling—The organization in charge of cycling in America. It makes the rules, sanctions the events, and licenses the competitors.

Upstroke—When a rider is pulling up on a pedal.

Velodrome—An indoor or outdoor track for bicycle racing with banked turns and flat straightaways. Usually made of wood (indoors) or concrete (outdoors).

Wheels—Your bike.

Wind Up—Steady acceleration designed to peak with an all-out effort.

United States Olympic Committee
Sports Series

This unique United States Olympic Committee Sports Series now offers eight new titles! Each book in this series is geared toward the beginner but all provide useful information for Olympic fans of all levels. Best of all, part of the purchase price of each book will directly support the activities of the U.S. Olympic Team.

Fill out the form on the back of this page to order by mail, fax or telephone.

Griffin Publishing

United States Olympic Committee
Sports Series Order Form
(Please print):

Date:_____

Name: _____

Address: _____

City:_____State:____Zip: ____

Phone:(___) _____

Title	Price	Qty / Amount
A Basic Guide to Archery	$7.95	____/_____
A Basic Guide to Badminton	$7.95	____/_____
A Basic Guide to Cycling	$7.95	____/_____
A Basic Guide to Decathlon	$8.95	____/_____
A Basic Guide to Equestrian	$7.95	____/_____
A Basic Guide to Soccer	$7.95	____/_____
A Basic Guide to Wrestling	$7.95	____/_____
Olympism	$8.95	____/_____

Subtotal: _____

8.25% tax (CA only): _____

S/H charges:
1 title $2.50
each additional title $1.00

S/H: _____

Total: _____

Send this order form with payment (check, money order or credit card info), to the address at the right.

Griffin Publishing
544 W. Colorado Street
Glendale, CA 91204

Credit cards: VISA or MasterCard only.
(circle one) **VISA   MC**

Account number _____

Expiration date ___/___

Signature _____

For faster service on credit card orders call 1-818-244-1470 or Fax 1-818-244-7408.